IT'S *Free Write* FRIDAY!

PALMETTO
PUBLISHING
Charleston, SC
www.PalmettoPublishing.com

Copyright © 2024 by Meagan Wagner, Ed.D.

All rights reserved

No portion of this book may be reproduced, stored in a retrieval system, or transmitted in any form by any means–electronic, mechanical, photocopy, recording, or other–except for brief quotations in printed reviews, without prior permission of the author.

Paperback ISBN: 979-8-82295-739-8

IT'S *Free Write* FRIDAY!

A simple routine with a profound impact

Meagan Wagner, Ed.D.

For all passionate educators in South Carolina and beyond, who make the most profound impact on our world every day despite so many difficulties in our profession.

Contents

Acknowledgements	1
Introduction: What is Free Write Friday?	3
Chapter One: Accountability	5
Chapter Two: Benefits	9
Chapter Three: Implementation	13
Chapter Four: Impact	29
Chapter Five: Frequently Asked Questions	31
Extras	36
References	44

Acknowledgements

A page of words would never be enough to thank my husband, Michael, for the encouragement, love, support, patience, and feedback on this and every other dream I have envisioned for myself and for our family. Thank you for believing in me every step of the way. I must acknowledge my four precious boys. Luke and Noah, you are the best helpers in everything. Thank you for doing more than your fair share of the family chores and for bringing in the crate of notebooks each weekend. Your help in every aspect of our busy life keeps me sane. Joey and Will, you are my sweet cuddle bugs and biggest fans. Thank you for always reminding me that I am loved. I hope I have shown all four of you to never give up on any dream you have. I love you all so much.

Thank you to my parents, Lonnie and Sue. Your support and encouragement in every endeavor is unmatched. I know I am a phone call away from any guidance or reassurance I need. To my in-laws, Scott and Suzy, thank you for always being willing to help in whatever the need may be. Thank you to my very best friend, Stephanie, for endless love and for always cheering me on.

Thank you to my colleagues throughout my career. To my neighboring teachers, who lovingly tolerate our Friday cheers (and sometimes shout back!). To my teacher besties, who have implemented FWF in their own classrooms and supported me at district or state presentations: Cindy Armstrong, Hannah Bodony, Susan Censoplano, Mary Margaret Delap, Janessa Dixon, Meghan Elvington, Karen Erickson, Tracy Fowler, Heather Greene, Joy Hardy, April Harmon, Daisha Hennicken, Jillian Hoffman, Alexis Kingry, Jake Lassow, Tarin Lewis, Jen McGraw, Meghan Pavelka, MaryBeth Rush, Dr. Allison Thompson, and SO many more (forgive me if I missed someone!). It means the world to me that you all have supported me in one way or another in the hardest job in the world. To my current administration, including but not limited to Jessie Bolton, Darah Huffman, Jonathan Sierputowski, Katie Smith, and so many more: thank you for celebrating FWF and appreciating its value from the get-go.

Finally, thank you to every educator (although English teachers are my FAVORITE). Your work matters. You are changing the world through every student you impact. Never forget that.

Introduction:
What is Free Write Friday?

Well? It is exactly what it sounds like: students are free to write whatever they want. Defined nearly forty years ago, "Free writing is geared towards self-discovery or exploration of a topic, usually having students write about whatever interests them in the form of personal journals or sketches that will be shared with others" (Fox and Suhor, p.34). Kwame Alexander (2019) identifies the importance of free writing, saying it "is both a source of inspiration and a steppingstone to self-enlightenment" (p. 46). End of introduction. Just kidding.

  Sounds easy, right? Like why even read the rest of this book? In my eighteen years as a secondary English educator, Free Write Friday (FWF) is the one routine that remains in my pedagogical practice every single year, regardless of what level or grade I am teaching. However, the routine itself has evolved over time. The result is what I believe to be the single most powerful routine for *any* English classroom. Teachers of composition or creative writing electives? This one's for you, too.

  This book will show you *how* to make a simple routine effective and impactful in your own classrooms. Interspersed throughout are what I call *fine print admissions*: those asides strictly admitting something related to the topic for context and understanding. Think of these as the comments I would say directly to you, face to face, as we wait for the copy machine to stop grunting and start copying. They are quick, honest, and *hopefully* pretty helpful.

Chapter One: Accountability explores the nitty gritty elements like rules, grading, responses, and more. Chapter Two: Benefits establishes how FWF creates connections, improves behavior, provides social and emotional learning opportunities, and so much more. Honestly, the whole book touches on the benefits and still won't cover them all. You'll discover surprising benefits upon implementation. Chapter Three: Implementation goes beyond the rules to help you establish this routine in an effective manner, including variations to choose from so it best suits your needs and those of your students. If, by the end of chapter three, you don't already see the impact of FWF, then chapter four spells it out for you with anecdotes and student writing samples to illustrate its power. Chapter Five addresses frequently asked questions --- both from students and educators -- to provide a complete understanding of how it works. And trust me: Free Write Friday *works*, if done well. Hence, the guidelines provided in this book.

Ring the cowbell, y'all: It's free write Friday!

Chapter One:
Accountability

Before we dive into holding students accountable for writing, I want to paint the picture of what a typical FWF looks like. Setting: Average public high school classroom on a Friday morning. I stand in the hall, ringing a cowbell and greeting students with variations of "You know what day it is!" and "That's right!" and "Yass queen! Can't wait to read the next chapter of your story!" Students are entering classrooms for first block. As soon as the tardy bell rings, I run into the classroom and shout, "Hey y'all! It's Free Write Friday!" My students clap, cheer, shout, and stomp. Free Write Friday is a celebration.

"Happy Friday!" I state, walking to the Promethean board to go over the agenda. "As you can see, today we have Free Write time, a vocab quiz, and then a mini-Socratic seminar on *Things Fall Apart*! [Switching slides from agenda to ideas]. Open up your notebooks to the next available page of your Writing section! Here are your ideas for the week! Remember, I'd much rather read *your* own ideas! But if you get stuck, responding to one of these is an option. As always, look back at my previous responses for more inspiration. Happy writing!" I hit play on our class Spotify playlist, switch from Slides to my document camera, and begin to write in my notebook as my students begin to write in theirs. End scene.

It really is that simple, but there is a fine line between balancing accountability and the freedom of free writing. You know how reading logs, reading responses, and book projects are killing students' love of reading (*Readicide,* as Kelly Gallagher calls it)? Well text dependent analysis, citing evidence, and traits rubrics are killing students' love of writing: which I will, obviously, call *writeicide.* Gallagher and Kittle (2014) suggest "Teachers are making a critical error when they focus on writing for tasks only" (p. 15). The primary goal of Free Write Friday is to provide students a pathway back to enjoying writing again.

Just as low stakes and choice are resurrecting a love of reading, the same can happen for writing. My go-to approach for most of my classes is simple, low stakes, and choice-driven: ten sentences or more of authentic and original writing gets you a 100. In my lower-level classes, I often say "Just do the things!" and this is one of those things. Through the tasks I assign them, my students are learning and growing. While certain constrained, standards-based writing tasks do have their time and place within our classrooms, so does freedom. A balance of both will build effective and motivated writers.

Now, are you sitting down? Because I need you to prepare yourself for this next and *most* important element of accountability for FWF: I do not grade grammar or spelling. I think the importance of this caveat is clear, so please don't start a hashtag movement against me. Fellow grammarians, I am one of you. A passionate fighter for the Oxford comma. A teacher of parallelism, semicolons, and homophones. I promise my students get their dose of conventions instruction. Just not on Fridays. *Please*. Not. On. Fridays.

(**Fine print admission #1**: If I have a writer who consistently makes the same grammatical mistake in several free writes, I *may* jot him or her a quick note about it. It really is hard to pass up the teachable moment. Does that make you feel better? But I do so within a compliment sandwich: "Wow! I LOVE the imagery in this! Their = pronoun and they're is your contraction of they are. And GIRL! Their friendship is already so well-developed! Relatable! Love it!" Now I only do this very rarely.)

That compliment sandwich brings me to the next and equally important element of FWF accountability: responses. I read every single FWF and I write back to every single student. Do not skip this crucial step, or the powerful impact will not occur. I have taught in Southwest Ohio, the Lowcountry, and upstate South Carolina. Eight schools, grades six through twelve. Here is what I observed: students are the same everywhere. And they want to be seen and heard. Writing back makes them feel both. In chapter three, I provide some tips for not drowning in burnout from these responses alone. Responding to every student is possible and of utmost importance. Suffice it to say, your responses matter exponentially. In addition to my personal responses, each writer also receives a sticker in the Mail Pocket of their Reader-Writer-Notebook. More on this in chapter three, as well.

(**Fine print admission #2**: I spend entirely too much time choosing the perfect sticker for each student, based on what they wrote or what I know about them. It is fun for me and they love it.)

Free writes are certain free game for future writing lessons, revisions, and workshops. "When we free write, we just let our words out, all of them. And while some of what we write may just be the sludge necessary to clear out before the treasure unfolds, we also may go back and read what we wrote and find a shining nugget that we can use for later writing" (Alexander, 2019, p. 46). Kittle and Gallagher (2014), state "The balance between practice with features (like dialogue) and freewriting is key. Writing every day in notebooks does not mean teaching a technique every day; it means getting students in the habit of transferring thinking into words and sentences" (p. 36). My students do all sorts of writing in their RWN: prompt-based writing, notes, one-pagers, lists, quick writes, and more. So free writes are just additional entries among many other types of writing and therefore, definitely usable for specific writing work later in the semester. They may even become the mentor text or passage study of a future lesson. Just do not remove the freedom, low stakes, choice of those Fridays. Okay? Promise?

If ten sentences is not going to work for you, do it differently! Some students easily write a page or more every Friday, so that could be your only parameter. Students could choose from many free writes to eventually revise, edit, and publish for a grade instead of weekly grades. Just avoid *writeicide*, so consider your grading choices deeply.

Or.

    Or.

        Or.

Don't grade them at all! Feedback / personal response is *so* much more effective than grading, anyway. But I digress…

However you choose to account for your student writing, keep it low stakes, choice-oriented, and focused on regrowing a love of writing.

Chapter Two: *Benefits*

The benefits of Free Write Friday are indeed endless, but I will focus on connection and growth. Have you ever gone the whole semester or year with a student, only to find out during the last week that...they have a job at your favorite restaurant or love your Chicago Cubs? Free Write Friday allows you to build individual connections and positive rapport with every single student. With the angry student. The silent-but-brilliant student. The frequently absent student. You get the point. Can't you see? The potential is so great, it is worth the time.

Because of the connections made from FWF, I do not typically have many behavior issues in my classroom. On rare occasions, a student does make a poor choice in class. But I usually have some context thanks to his or her previous free writes and I have, several times, then received a heartfelt apology in a subsequent free write. Also, because of these connections, my students want to do well for me. They know I care and often say as much. My high stakes, state mandated assessments always glean very high pass rates among my students. Near the testing weeks, students are often writing about their concerns and worries about the upcoming assessments. This provides a great opportunity for me to build their confidence in my individual responses to them.

Am I honestly claiming that this simple, weekly routine could positively impact behavior, motivation, engagement, and academic success? Does an English teacher own cardigans? The answer is, obviously, yes.

At first, you will read a *lot* of free writes on "what I'm doing this weekend". This is totally normal and you do learn things about your students through these. As the weeks progress, you will learn about students' passions, worries, and dreams. "Through writing poems, stories, journals, and freewriting, they gain comfort with written language and with themselves" (Collins, 1990, p. 655). You'll read hilarious or frightening fiction that develops further each Friday. Many free writes will, eventually, break your empathetic-teacher-heart into a thousand pieces.

Students will open up, once you've built trust and made that connection with them. They will report situations of abuse, homelessness, trauma. Sometimes, the FWF responses that I write provide the opportunity to check on those students who might be exhibiting red flags like social withdrawal and sudden, declining grades. For the love of all things educational, give them that 100 and get them help. After working with my administration and guidance team to fill out the obligatory reports, I often find myself thinking "what if they didn't have FWF as their outlet / lifeline?" That thought frightens me.

Humble-brag moment: my FWF routine touched upon social emotional learning long before it was cool. My students use free writes to discuss their new self-awareness as they mature from their previous, middle school selves. They write about the observations of cliques or relationships in the cafeteria or on buses. "Because adolescence is a time of self-consciousness, personal writing allows adolescents to explore their perceptions and feelings" (Collins, 1990, p. 655). They ask for advice and explore big decisions in writing. They learn that it is okay to feel however they feel and they should practice the pause of thinking and processing it. There are times in the semester when it seems like every student writes about how stressed they are: how many tests they have coming up and what is going on at home. Their ability to communicate these factors is already helping them grow as individuals. I ensure my responses always encourage them and help their emotional well-being thrive.

Across the front of my classroom in large letters, it says *writing is thinking*. I also say it all the time in my lessons on annotating or while they are responding to a prompt or quick write. It amazes me to discover what students are thinking about in these free writes. More importantly, it helps me to see how they are growing personally and academically.

Students who cared about not knowing anyone at the beginning of the semester write about their clubs or lunch with friends at the end of the semester. Students who focused on learning their schedule at the beginning are discussing their post-secondary hopes and dreams by the end. Students who began their first free writes with "I'm not sure what to write about..." are pouring Nobel-worthy poetry onto the page in the late weeks of the semester. It is powerful for students to see how their own thinking has changed and matured, even within one semester. Indeed, as Kim Stover (1988) put it, "writers become consciously aware of their unconscious voices; they would realize that, yes, they did have something to say, after all" (p. 62).

While the grade expectation of ten sentences is simple, I do not typically have to count sentences and neither do my students. Once they are writing originally and authentically, they write way more than ten sentences. They are pouring that thinking onto the page. Even more powerful is that I have observed their other writings are more thoughtful, organized, and in-depth. In my humble opinion, this is because we practice thinking through writing every Friday. So yes, additional benefits to FWF include building writing stamina and growing confidence as authentic and original thinkers.

Remember that compliment sandwich? Another benefit of FWF is that you will innately observe student deficits in writing and, therefore, identify specific writing lesson needs. If I observe that many writers are still confusing *their*, *they're*, and *there* in their free writes then I am most certainly going to address that in a minilesson, station, or review later. Free writes can inform instruction as pre-assessments or even as formative assessments in an official capacity. To clarify, I mean this: give them the 100 while also gleaning the information to further guide instruction.

Free Write Friday provides an avenue for our writers to be the star. Our athletes and musicians are often in the limelight of the school's Facebook page or website, but we do not have a student writing magazine or anything of the like. Writing could be a student's big talent and they deserve to be in the limelight, too. After the trust and celebratory nature of implementation has been established (see chapter three), these students become rock stars within the classroom. Quickly, peers will learn who the great writers within the room are and you will watch those writers bloom into confident captains of the industry, so to speak. Please give them that opportunity! It might just change their lives.

I'll end this chapter on one of the unexpected benefits of FWF: professional impact. As someone who has taught at eight different schools, Free Write Friday is my go-to answer for many interview questions as an applicant for a new position. It checks so many boxes. How do I build rapport with my students? How do I combat student apathy? How do I handle more challenging students? How do I manage behaviors? The answer to all of these and more is Free Write Friday.

Chapter Three: *Implementation*

You can see why a low stakes accountability approach is so important to gleaning the many benefits of Free Write Friday. Equally important is *how* you implement this routine, beginning on the very first Friday with a room full of fresh faces. In this chapter, I will share the celebratory nature of my approach and specific tips for ensuring effectiveness.

Every Friday, I enter / jump / glide / zoom into my classroom and shout: "It's Free Write Friday!" to which my generous teenagers humor me in varied, celebratory responses. They stomp, cheer, clap, and shout. They pound on their desks. Yes, some of them roll their eyes. But they are smiling even before it quiets down. By week three or four, those eye rollers are participating in the exuberant cheering. If I forget to lead the shouts as I enter the classroom, they will quickly call me out on my misstep. Or, one of my students will run up front, grab my cowbell, and lead it themselves. Years ago, a student bought me a cowbell for the occasion and it has since become a symbol of the excitement and a reminder that we are about to scream and shout. In school. And we are allowed?!

While introducing Free Write Friday, (on what I call FWF Launch Day), I first provide my students with the simple grading expectation and then list Can Dos and Can't Dos:

Can Dos:
- Get creative and try different writing styles
- Ask for help thinking of a topic
- Write poetry, fiction, or letters
- Write an ongoing chapter book
- Write about your hopes and dreams
- Tell me what is going on in your life outside of school
- Change topics by creating new paragraphs
- Report abuse or ask for help but I WILL get you help

Can't Dos:
- Include inappropriate language or bullying toward others
- Repeat the same sentence ten times
- Separate random fragments with periods to make it look like 10 sentences
- Write a bunch of simple, brainless sentences
- Write down the lyrics to your favorite song
- Write about other teachers (unless it is 100% positive)

Then, I share the following three example free writes with them, challenging them to decide whether each entry should be celebrated or revised.

(**Fine print admission #3**: I used to call these *The Good, the Bad, and the Ugly*. But great writing often starts out bad or ugly and I didn't want to send the wrong message. So, *Celebrate or Revise?* it is.)

Here is what a typical class discussion sounds like for this part of the introduction lesson:

Dr. Wagner: Alright, writers. Now that you know what Free Write Friday is all about, we are going to look at a few examples. I want you to guess whether each piece of writing should be celebrated or if it needs revised. Think about the requirements of FWF! Ready?

Example 1:

    This is my first FWF and I think I am going to like them. I hate how we never get to write what we WANT to write in school anymore. It is always a required topic or prompt. We never get to write stories like we did when we were in lower grades. I used to love writing but then I began to hate it because we had to write so many essays.

    So far, I like all my classes. The teachers seem cool and the subjects aren't too hard. I miss the middle school, though. It was easier to find my way around. I never see my close friends. All my classes now are with people I don't really know. My mom says that is a good thing – it will expand my horizons or whatever, but I don't think so.

Dr. Wagner: So? Celebrate or revise?

Students: (usually with uncertainty) Celebrate?

Dr. Wagner: Yes! Great job, courageous thinkers. I see many sentences. Remember, writing is thinking! I now know what this new student of mine is thinking about. It is original and authentic. Notice the topics can change. Whatever is on your mind, just write! Now, for the next example. Celebrate or revise?

Example 2:
I hate school. School is stupid. School is boring. I don't learn. Learning is stupid. I am tired. I just want to go home. I am done.

Students: (before I even ask) Revise!

Dr. Wagner: (with snoring noises) Yes, please give me more. I read and write back, remember? I know more is going on in your brain than that so give it to me straight! I'd rather you complain openly on why you HATE school than just write in those choppy, short sentences. This is where authenticity is important. Alright, example 3:

Example 3:

When I picture my hometown, there's a bronze spray-tanned statue of you and a plaque underneath it that threatens to push me down the stairs at our school. And it was always the same searing pain. But I dreamed that one day, I could say all that time you were throwing punches. I was building something. And I can't forgive the way you made me feel... but I can't forget the way you made me heal. And it wasn't a fair fight, or a clean kill each time that Aimee stomped across my grave. And then she wrote headlines in the local paper, laughing at each baby step I'd take.

While I read that one and display it on the screen, my Swifties immediately giggle. Others catch on and look around.

Dr. Wagner: Well? Celebrate or revise?

Student: Revise! It's a song!!!

Dr. Wagner: Yes, thank you, Swifties. While this does sound like a Free Write, it is not your original and authentic writing. It is Taylor's original and authentic writing. Anyway, what you could do instead here is tell me *why* "ThanK You, AIMee" is stuck in your head. Why is it important? Tell me *that* and you have a free write!" I pause, assessing their facial expressions. "Fun fact: many famous singer / songwriters began by putting their own free writes to music! Any questions before we write our first entries? Alright, happy writing!" End scene.

I usually show a fourth example, which is a great start of fictional writing with atrocious spelling. While some are quick to want to revise it, others catch on and shout out "Celebrate!" Then I confirm and have them explain why. It is a great story with characterization, a hook, and introduction to a conflict. Students experience a reminder and affirmation that spelling does not matter but authentic and original writing does. For that and the previous examples in one handout, check out the *Extras* at the end of the book!

I typically allot about 25 minutes of writing time within a 90-minute-blocked class. I know your eyes just went wide but I promise you it is time well spent. As with every routine, students who are done early may read independently, but most of them just keep writing once they are in the routine. The first few Fridays, that much time is needed to give students time to think, pause, write, repeat. Occasionally, we fall way behind in a content-heavy week and I shorten FWF time. The students moan and groan when I tell them they only have ten or fifteen minutes to pour it out. But I remind them that they can always come back to a free write and add to it later.

The tips below are invaluable to practice every Friday and especially on Launch Day for long term effectiveness and impact:

Tip #1: Model the Practice

It is sound and best practice to model reading, writing, and thinking. On FWF Launch Day, I use my document camera and allow my students to watch my process. I model the struggle of writing. I scribble out mistakes. I start over. I change topics. I stare into space to think for a moment before continuing. If I'm going to be vulnerable and share my writing with them, they become more willing to do so with me.

> FWF 8/15/21
>
> Another school year has kicked off and I already love my students! My classes are a bit talkative, but they're working hard, too! That's my kind of class!
>
> UGH. We spent our entire planning period in a meeting about the new hall pass system. It seems a little bit confusing AND maybe even time consuming? But if it keeps my students safer, then I'm in.
>
> OMG. A student from last semester just stopped by to bring me a gift! She gave me Harry Potter stickers! SQUEAL! I can't wait to put a few on my notebook. And desk. And water bottle! Ooh and podium. Stickers are my love language. Can that be a thing? I think its a thing.

Tip #2: Write Back

    I believe the importance of this one has already been established, but it is worth emphasizing again. Students catch on when we don't read their writing (or whatever it is they turned in). I write personalized, short responses on every single free write. It becomes easy very quickly, I promise. You will quickly discern what students usually write about. You will know a made-up story immediately or a stream-of-consciousness entry. My comments are usually as simple as "Last week WAS odd with the testing schedule -- I am glad it is over, too!" or "I feel this on a deep level. You are so wise!"

IT'S *Free Write* FRIDAY!

> **Free-Write Friday**
>
> My tears are mistaken for weakness so I no longer cry.
>
> I let my emotions bottled up turn into anger. Instead of showing my emotions, I wrap it with bandages like they are my wounds to distract me from my feelings.
>
> *I bottle it up sometimes, too. ✓ WRITE IT OUT! It helps me.*

    Keeping up with the responses can be daunting, but I believe you will grow to enjoy it. Typically, I try to work on them immediately. I can knock out a full class (on average, 25 students) within about 20 - 30 minutes. That includes recording their score, writing a response, and spending entirely too much time gifting them with a cleverly chosen sticker. I do bring their Reader-Writer-Notebooks home on the weekends as needed, especially at the beginning, to ensure I keep up with the demand. Establishing the idea that I really do read them and write back is that important to me. My own children are used to helping unload my teacher cart from my beat up, soccer mom minivan.

    Taking the writings home is not necessary, however. I'm right there with you: *time* is always a problem. Never enough time to grade. Never enough time to plan. Never enough time to teach all the standards. I agree and feel the same way. And yet FWF is still worth my time. Establish a routine that you know you can handle. Three blocks? Rotate one block each Friday so you are only reading one class per week. I have seen teachers implement the practice of only grading one a month: students sticky-note which one they want the teacher to read and grade. If this is an easier way to start out, then try that. I believe that you will quickly see the worth of reading and responding.

Another strategy is to plan your Mondays as skills reviews or stations and try to multitask: responding while students work. If I can do a full class in twenty uninterrupted minutes, you might be able to do a full class in that ninety minute block while also managing the classroom and teaching the task. I am convinced that it helps for the students to observe me reading entries, smiling, choosing a sticker, and writing a personal note back. Let them see that from time to time.

Recall that some students will write very emotional and time-sensitive entries. For this reason, I always say "If you want me to read it right away, place it on my desk before you leave!" I even put it on my projected slides. Some teachers have a special basket on their desk for this purpose as another visual reminder. Otherwise, my students all place their RWNs in the basket labeled for their block. If there is a student who has exhibited some concerning behaviors throughout the week, I wait until they have left the room and then I check their writing.

(**Fine print admission #4:** I skim read. Fast. And once I get to know a writer -- I skim *some* more than others. Seconds perusing the page and then writing a quick comment about their story. Responding to every writer *is* attainable.)

Tip #3: Establish a Culture of Celebration and Sharing

If the cowbell and shouts were not explicit enough, launching FWF with a celebratory approach is paramount. Students finally get to write what they want! YAY! Sharing free writes is a part of what makes it so special. I give students the option to share in a variety of ways: read it, talk about what you wrote, read a part of it, or have the teacher read it! Anyone who shares out gets to pick out a sticker!

Since they watched me write on the document camera, I usually talk about my own writing briefly before prompting sharers.

Once, my students had just come from a motivational speaker on emotional health so many of them wrote about that in their free writes. This particular student surprised me, pouring a reaction onto the page within minutes:

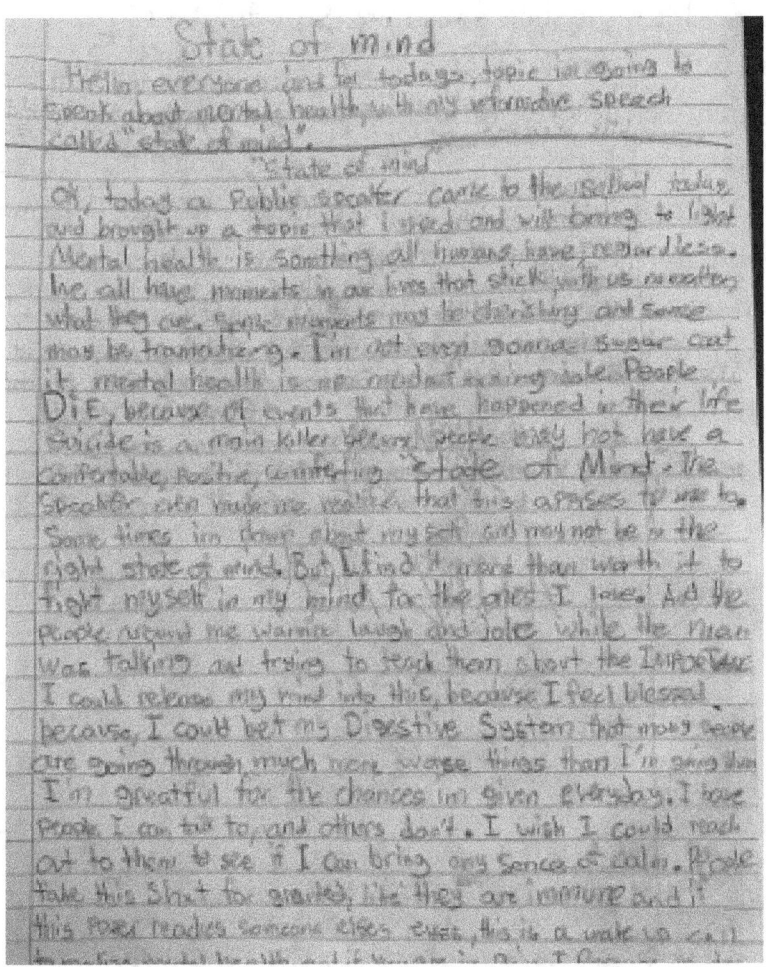

Even more surprising, was that he looked it over once and then raised his hand to share out. His passion for mental health was evident and he made us all laugh and cry. He states "I would bet my digestive system that many people are going through much more worse things than I'm going through". As I told him that day, this was one of the best lines I had ever read. Confusing syntax aside, this writer really changed the trajectory of our classroom community by sharing his reactions to the public speaker. Many students nodded and grunted in agreement to his synthesis.

Often, while writing, a student will come up to me and say "you wanna read it?" and of course they already know I'm *going* to read it. But they very obviously want me to read it right then and there. So I do. And I do so with acting that could earn an Oscar. I laugh out loud or shout "WHAT?!" and go to extremes to ensure that student gets the response they wanted. I'll say "you should read this to the class!" or "can I read this part to the class? It's amazing!" This slowly leads to more and more sharing. Just you wait. Poetry. Short stories. Personal stories about adoption. Connections because so-and-so is ALSO adopted! The class community grows closer and closer every Friday. And we clap, cheer, shout after every single sharer. My neighboring teachers must hate me.

Celebrations can occur in other ways, too. One colleague created a large Free Write Friday poster that she hangs above the door. Every Friday, the kids have to jump and high-five the poster on their way in. I love it! Even the students who are less than enthused end up smiling at the task. Another takes her writers outside to the courtyard every time weather allows. Instead of sharing every Friday, another means of celebration is to plan poetry slams or reading performances for extra credit.

Tip #4: Give Prompt Ideas

Yes, this contradicts everything in the rest of the book, but hear me out. This tip only developed in the last couple years. Let's call it Post-Covid Writer's Block. As you know, our students' stamina is lower than ever. They are not used to thinking for themselves (or at all, sometimes). Coming up with a topic on Friday was proving difficult for many of my students. So I tried offering an idea off the top of my head. I said, "write a story about getting locked in the gym with no phones or contact to the outside world. What happens?" Students smirked or looked at me judgmentally but I read some pretty great stories. This evolved into optional prompts offered every Friday.

The prompts I come up with are very clearly optional. I also make it abundantly clear that I would rather read the students' own thinking or topic over my topics, any day. But it has helped struggling students write more. It has helped burnt out students write after a day full of tests. (Why do we always end up testing on Fridays?!) I think of prompts on my drive in to work, during class throughout the week, or when something random and unexpected happens.

One time, everyone came to class talking a bit too much and a bit too loudly. Even their cheers for Free Write Friday were louder than normal. When I asked what was going on, they told me about the cat in the cafeteria. One precious freshman decided to rescue a stray cat who appeared at the bus stop. The student placed the cat in his backpack and brought it to school. Once he entered the cafeteria for free breakfast, chaos ensued. The cat got out and panicked, running across tables and under tables. So did, allegedly, the principal who engaged in the chase. So of course, I told them to write about it! Pens and pencils flew across the pages at lightning speed.

I wish I had kept those free writes. I remember them vividly, more than a decade later. It was a phenomenal lesson in perspective, in point of view (or it would have been, had I kept these free writes as mentor texts!). I read one from my quiet student, who thought she had heard meows on the bus and now it all made sense. I read several from students observing the chaos of the cafeteria at different angles and in different depths of imagery. I read a creative piece from the voice and perspective of that poor cat (who was pompous and judgmental of the foolish freshie who brought her into a measly high school). WHY DID I NOT KEEP THESE?! Anyway, moving on.

Another time, I came in on a Friday disheveled and upset. I was not my usual cheerful, cowbell-ringing self. The students noticed. I explained that my husband's car had been broken into during the night and it had upset me. I am a mom of four boys and we live in a safe neighborhood, but goodness I was not okay that day. The only thing stolen were his AirPods (THAT was the most appalling detail for my students). They asked "can we write about that?" and I quickly responded "sure! Insult the thief for me! That'll cheer me up!"

As a result, I read some of the most supportive and encouraging, spiteful and polite insults ever. My students had my back. I pity the fool who ever tries that again. Letters to the thief, rants on my behalf, and reasons I am the last person who should fall victim to thievery ensued. "I hope you step on a lego" and "I hope your pillow is never cold, even when you flip it!" paved the way for more and more hilarious entries. I think nearly EVERY student shared out that day. And I was, indeed, cheered up.

My optional prompts have also become an avenue for me to figure out things about my students. It may be questions like "what advice would you give to an upcoming student entering my class on day one?" or "WHY do some of you sleep during the state test? I know it is untimed but COME ON! That stresses me out!" and I end up reading really insightful responses. But I always emphasize that I'd rather read their original topics any day they can think of them. These prompt ideas just provide a scaffolding that their tired brains sometimes need. On any given Friday, I only provide two or three ideas. If you are a user of Flocabulary, their Week in Rap is also a great idea generator: it gives students many current events to write about and they often have very strong opinions for these. For a short list of some of my favorite, go-to ideas throughout the year, see the *Extras* at the end of the book!

Tip #5: Give Reluctant Writers Grace

Recall that my number one priority is for students to love writing again. Therefore, if a reluctant writer only writes a few sentences, your response could make or break that goal for the rest of the semester. There are several ways to handle this, depending on the student.

If you have easily seen ten or more sentences of writing from this student in other assignments (or otherwise have discerned that he or she is fully capable), then maybe a 30 out of 100 for three sentences is fair. I would definitely ask in my response "Are you okay? You did not write much and that is not like you. Tell me more about the football game!" Students do occasionally just find it too difficult to write. It is usually rare once they have acquired individual buy-in from the trust and connection with me.

Other solutions include:
- Interviewing the student verbally and counting their answers as sentences.
- Offering them time to write more, later, when they seem to be feeling better.
- Chat informally with them and model how their thinking is totally acceptable as sentences on the page (actually write what they say down!) This is especially effective as you end up getting to ten very quickly based on what they say.
- Celebrate growth, no matter how small. "Six sentences this week, after three last week? Great job! Look how much you are growing!"

However you respond, ensure you do it with the goal in mind. Still focus on connection and trust. They deserve a response just as much as the kid who wrote three pages.

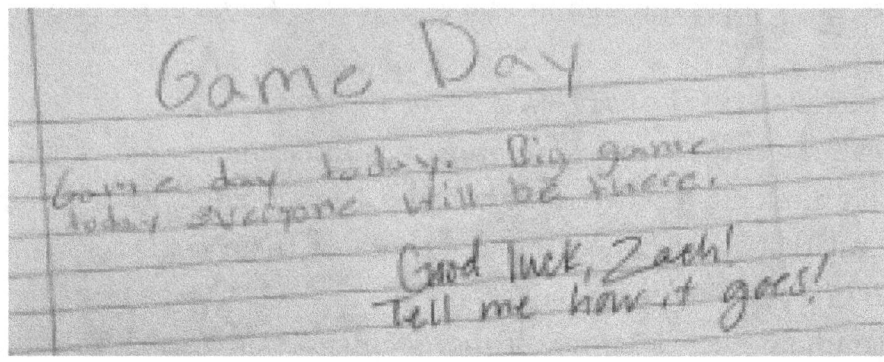

While I believe those Tips for Effectiveness are the unofficial edicts (is that an oxymoron?!) for successful implementation, there is one last element that I feel is important to share: the use of composition books. The use of my Reader-Writer-Notebooks is nearly as impactful as the aforementioned tips, so I divulge the details of how I use them here.

Most of my students' work throughout the semester goes into their RWNs and they are housed in my classroom, unless a writer chooses to take it home. As a teacher in South Carolina, I receive a supply check at the start of each school year to purchase classroom items. Between this and frequent PTA grants, I am usually able to provide a composition book to every student on the first day of class. This has become an important part of establishing a classroom that will read and write a great volume, starting on day one.

On the first day of class, I guide every student through RWN setup. We tape the first two pages together on the side and bottom to create a mail pocket. This is where I place handouts they missed while absent, stickers, notes, seat time notices that were in my box, and papers I found on the floor with their name on them. Students love checking their mail pocket when they get into class, especially on a Monday after FWF!

Directly after the Mail Pocket, the entire first half of these composition books is the Writing section. This section encompasses free writes, quick writes, prompt-based writings, passage studies, model texts, and handouts from writing lessons. It is a little bit interactive notebook and a lotta bit growing portfolio.

In the second half of the RWN, we have the Reading section (30 pages) and the Vocab section (20 pages). The former includes comprehension work, responses to reading, brainstorm lists, analysis handouts, annotation guides, and more. Academic terms, routine vocabulary work, and application of learned words in writing fit well into the Vocab section.

Being able to see all of their previous free writes allows me to go back and reference things I read. It allows me to differentiate according to needs I observe. It allows me to engage them through connecting to the interests I learn about. I can better recommend independent reading choices to readers because of what I see in their notebooks. When I teach inquiry, students often get to choose their own topics and often struggle with that autonomy. I am able to confer with them, flipping through their RWN, to suggest potential topics of interest to them.

Before an IEP meeting, I often flip through that student's RWN beforehand so I can discuss their growth as a reader and writer. I used to just have students write on a loose leaf piece of paper and I'll admit, a stack of 25 papers is way easier to take home than a stack of 25 composition books. However, the pros outweigh the cons and I prefer the RWNs. These notebooks become a representation of each student and evidence of how much they have learned within a semester.

Meagan Wagner, Ed.D.

Chapter Four: *Impact*

The saying goes "they won't remember what you said but they'll remember how you made them feel" and this is evident in Free Write Friday. My last major grade assignment for the year is a growth reflection assignment, in which students discuss their growth as a reader, writer, and thinker. They create slides to discuss their growth, citing examples from their RWNs. Additionally, they tell me about their growth in video form. Free writes, specifically, are almost always discussed in the slides and the videos. Students grow to love them, whether they realize it or not.

Free writing does not have to be on Friday and on a few occasions throughout my career, we had emergency free writes earlier in the week. Many of you have had the unfortunate experience of losing a student during the semester in which you teach them. One of my students passed away in a car accident during her sophomore year. The next day, I gave my students the option to free write. "You don't have to write about her. You don't have to write at all. But if you want to or need to, this time is yours." Every single student wrote and wrote and wrote. As did I. I still remember how life felt that day: heavy and impossible at the beginning, sad but possible by the end. Writing truly heals.

Free Write Friday impacts students beyond our time together. I have students who come back to me all the time stating they miss free writing so much! "We even asked Ms. So-and-So if we could do Free Write Friday, but she said no!" My response is always "what's stopping you from free writing?! You don't have to be in a classroom to do it!" I have students continue writing and sharing with me, long after they have finished my course. They will hand me a notebook as they walk by in the hall, or I will walk into my classroom to discover one has been slid under the door for my reading pleasure.

A few years ago, I was checking my teacher mailbox hoping for test scores and found, instead, a small gift bag. When I opened it, I exclaimed out loud and my eyes welled up with tears. It was a pair of earrings that said "Free Write Friday!" on them. They had to have been personally ordered from Etsy or the like, because I certainly did not see them on Amazon. That gift giver wrote that my connection with him through free writes helped him survive a semester in which he became medically homebound and struggled to keep up with the demands of school. I proudly wear them every Friday. Earrings might just be my love language (besides stickers)!

A few years ago, I had the pleasure of sharing my FWF routine with fellow educators at the South Carolina Council for Teachers of English's annual conference. Many of my colleagues attended my session to support me and have since implemented FWF in their classrooms. Students who are not mine will see me in the hallway and shout, "It's Free Write Friday!" New students entering my classroom often comment that they have heard of me or something like "Oh you're the one with the cowbell?" Administration has celebrated with us, teachers of other content areas have heard of it, and the Yearbook even did a half-page spread on FWF. If this is my legacy, then so be it. I am proud of what Free Write Friday does and will continue to do for our students, teachers, and classroom communities.

Chapter Five:
Frequently Asked Questions

I hope that the previous chapters have given you a deep understanding of the power that Free Write Friday can have. Here are some questions that I have received over the years from teachers like you and me.

What if my students won't write?

I address this in more depth in chapter three but I also want to add that, like many issues with our students, there is usually a deeper reason for a student's choices. Try to get to the core of the problem and explore *why* they do not want to write. Speaking with them one-on-one may provide the attention they were seeking. Conversely, that attention may be so unwanted, that they write from here on out to avoid it.

What if my administration / instructional leaders see FWF as a waste of instructional time?

Ohhhh goodness can I just say make them read this book? Just kidding, kind of. You could certainly reference the book. But you could also reference your standards. Free Write Friday implements several of our 2023 South Carolina College and Career Ready English Language Arts Standards (in this case, English 2 standards are referenced, as that is the majority of what I currently teach):

- ELA.E2.OE.1 Read and write for a variety of purposes, including academic and personal, for extended periods of time.
- ELA.E2.C.4: Demonstrate command of standard English grammar and conventions when writing.
- ELA.E2.C.6: Write independently and legibly for a variety of tasks and purposes.
- ELA.E2.C.7: Organize and communicate ideas through a range of formats to engage a variety of audiences.

There is no way to address those standards unless routine and systematic writing takes place in our classrooms. Words like *variety, personal, time, demonstrate, independently,* and *ideas* immediately stand out as prioritized elements of FWF. Who can argue with standards-based alignment?

What if I do not read and write back?

Let me be the first to tell you -- from repeated personal experience -- that the Monday that arrives before I have read and responded to Free Writes is a scary Monday, indeed. Well, scarier than a normal Monday. I observe my students picking up their RWNs and immediately flipping to read my commentary or checking their Mail Pocket for a sticker. While the disappointment in their faces is bad enough, it is the verbal students who make it worse. "Dr. Wagner! You didn't read our free writes?!"

I am sincerely apologetic, but it does happen. I have four boys in sports. I also prioritize mental health which sometimes means taking a break. "I'm so sorry! I cannot wait to read them. I will catch up this week. Remember, if you really want or need me to read it soon, place it on my desk! I love you!"

This brings me back to the point I made earlier: create a routine that you can handle. I know that most weeks of a semester, I am going to be able to prioritize those free writes because they mean the world to me.

IT'S *Free Write* FRIDAY!

> (**Fine print admission #5:** If I know ahead of time that I will be too burned out to address free writes, I have been guilty of administering a longer-than-normal vocab quiz or a collaborative activity that *unexpectedly* takes up the whole block. Did ya see me wink just then? Those Fridays are okay too: the students express their sadness that they did not have time to free write and that secretly boosts my burned-out ego about this whole routine.)

How do I build that deep trust with students to get them beyond writing about their weekends?

Great question. This one takes practice and experience. I first establish trust in my introductory launch. I tell my students "Nobody will read these but me, unless you choose to share them" and I stick to my word. I am the keeper of secrets. Mum's the word.

On occasion, a student will say something like: "Can I write Lainey a note in her RWN?" or something of the like. My response is always the same: "I'm sorry, but no! Just as I do not let *anyone* read your notebook, you may not read anyone else's unless they choose to let you." I'm actually grateful when this scenario comes up. That Oscar-award winning acting comes in handy again and I overemphasize my answer, ensuring everyone heard. I really do observe others listening in on my response. I believe it solidifies their trust in me.

Additionally, I build trust with my students by being vulnerable. In very short commentary, I relate to their struggles. I share my stories. I model struggle. I am one of them: a writer who pours it all on the page without worrying about spelling or grammar. Short phrases like "Tell me more about your girlfriend! I'm glad you're happy!" and "I was always a bad test-taker and I turned out okay! Do not worry! Your talents are plentiful in other areas" provide just enough context to express vulnerability and care.

My Professional Learning Community and I have to have our grades aligned and they do not want to do FWF, but I do. How do I proceed?

This is a great consideration to make. First and foremost, remember that you do not have to grade them. Receiving responses and stickers will slowly win over your students. If some do not write since it is not for a grade, give them that one-on-one attention or interview them verbally. Encourage them and connect with them in other ways. Slowly, I believe you will start to see some words on the page.

Can I have my students type their free writes?

When my students inevitably ask, "Can we just type them?", my answer is always and emphatically no. Students are on devices more than enough already and there is something to be said about putting pen to paper. In fact, in Gallagher's (2011) "Ten Core Beliefs About the Teaching of Writing" Core Belief #7 is: "Students should not lose the skill of writing by hand" (p.233).

Writing is thinking and thinking is messy. That mess is part of the process and that mess does not show up on the screen when students delete instead of scribble. I always give them the vague phrase "research shows" that handwriting is more powerful brain work than typing. If they have not handwritten much text in a while, they get over it quickly.

I have had many students over the years who had accommodations for typing longer written responses. Most of them chose to write in their notebooks instead. The few who truly needed to type them always did so quietly and appropriately. Then, I print them out and tape them into that student's RWN.

(**Fine print admission #6**: I cannot stand reading on the screen. I'm old, okay? So, if a digital RWN is something you wish to *try*, then go for it. And share your thoughts with me!)

What do I do about multi language learners?

My approach to explaining free write Friday to my multi language learners is the same as my approach for most of my content, routines, and activities: I type up an explanation of what we will be focusing on. Then, I use the translate tool to create a new copy of the document in each student's language. I print and deliver them confidentially via the students' Mail Pockets in the RWNs before the start of class. In Spring of 2024, I delivered my explanation in Spanish, Portuguese, and Korean to five precious students. Every one of them wrote in English. See the *Extras* for my Introduction to Free Write for Translation.

****

In closing, I hope that you'll give FWF a try and I hope it will impact your classroom and career as greatly as it has impacted mine. I would love to hear about your implementation and answer any questions you have. Please feel free to email me at meagan.wagner7@gmail.com. I will also share my launch introduction slides, photos, videos of shouting, and whatever else you think to ask me about. Happy Writing!

Extras

Provided on the ensuing pages are the basic handouts for implementation of FWF.

FWF Launch Materials: Introduction to FWF

What is Free Write Friday?

- You are free to write whatever you want, within reason.
- Your writing must be original.
- Your writing may be journaling, letter, poetry, fiction, summary, venting, etc.
- You are encouraged to explore various styles, forms, and topics in your writing.

How will it be graded?

- Ten or more original sentences of good quality, school-appropriate topics.
- Spelling is not graded! This allows you to "relax" and try to enjoy writing again.

What happens when I'm done writing?

- I will read and write back to you! You'll even get a sticker.
- You may read silently if you finish early.
- Students will be given the opportunity to share out but that will never be required! Some options for sharing:
    - Read the whole piece
    - Read an excerpt
    - Just tell us what you wrote about
    - Ask the teacher to read it aloud

FWF Launch Materials:
Can Do / Can't Do Lists

What you CAN DO in a FWF:

- Get creative and try different writing styles
- Ask for help thinking of a topic
- Write poetry, fiction, or letters
- Write an on-going chapter book
- Write about your hopes and dreams
- Tell me what is going on in your life outside of school
- Change topics by creating new paragraphs
- Report abuse or ask for help but I WILL get you help

What you CAN'T DO in a FWF:

- Include excessive inappropriate language or bullying toward others
- Repeat the same sentence ten times
- Separate random fragments with periods to make it look like 10 sentences
- Write a bunch of simple, brainless sentences
- Write down the lyrics to your favorite song
- Write about other teachers (unless it is 100% positive)

IT'S *Free Write* FRIDAY!

FWF Launch Materials:
Celebrate or Revise? Examples

Free Write 1: Celebrate or revise?

This is my first FWF and I think I am going to like them. I hate how we never get to write what we WANT to write in school anymore. It is always a required topic or prompt. We never get to write stories like we did when we were in lower grades. I used to love writing but then I began to hate it because we had to write so many essays.

So far, I like all my classes. The teachers seem cool and the subjects aren't too hard. I miss the middle school, though. It was easier to find my way around. I never see my close friends. All my classes now are with people I don't really know. My mom says that is a good thing – it will expand my horizons or whatever, but I don't think so.

Free Write 2: Celebrate or revise?

I hate school. School is stupid. School is boring. I don't learn. Learning is stupid. I am tired. I just want to go home. I am done.

Free Write 3: Celebrate or revise?

When I picture my hometown, there's a bronze spray-tanned statue of you and a plaque underneath it that threatens to push me down the stairs at our school. And it was always the same searing pain. But I dreamed that one day, I could say all that time you were throwing punches. I was building something. And I can't forgive the way you made me feel... but I can't forget the way you made me heal. And it wasn't a fair fight, or a clean kill each time that Aimee stomped across my grave. And then she wrote headlines in the local paper, laughing at each baby step I'd take.

Free Write 4: Celebrate or revise?

Onse upon a time, their was a dog named Leesi. Leesi was a very gud dog. She new how to run and fetch and play ball. Leesi was Jon's best freind. Leesi had blak spots on her wite ferr and a blak spot over her rite I. She was calm, loving, and loyul. She was also good with dureckshuns.

One day, Leesi went missing. She had run after a ball in the woods but did not re-uppear. Jon looked every were but couldn't find her. (to be continyood next FWF).

IT'S *Free Write* FRIDAY!

My Favorite Prompt Ideas for Writers Who Are Stuck:

Beginning of the semester / year prompts:

- All of you have beautiful and unique names. Tell me the meaning or story behind your name, if you know it!
- If you could choose one song to motivate you, represent you, or help you survive, what song would it be and why?
- Tell me the most unique things about yourself. Hobbies, family, interests, talents, memorable stories, scars, etc. are all great to discuss!
- What are you most excited about for this semester / year?
- How did you do last year / semester in your classes? What do you hope to achieve this semester / year?

Middle of the semester / year:

- Go back and look at your first few FWFs. What do you notice? Have you changed as a writer? As a human?
- To the tune of Bon Jovi: "Ohhhhh we're halfway there!" What are you most proud of in class so far? What do you wish you had done better?
- What has been the most difficult aspect of English class so far for you?
- Your Croc charms have all suddenly come alive. Tell the story.
- How did you feel about Spirit Week? If you were in charge, what would you do differently?

- Happy Halloween! Change the entire school into a haunted walkthrough experience for the brave. Describe what it would look like!

End of the semester / year:

- It is testing day. None of us are allowed to have our phones in the room. The power goes out. The doors lock automatically. We have no way out and no means of communication. What happens?!
- Write a letter to next year's students, on how to survive English! What tips would you give them?
- Dr. Wagner always says, "*Writing is thinking!*" and "*Just do the things*!" Which one of these mantras was most helpful and applicable to you this year? Why?

Free Write Friday Introduction – in Translations

Free Write Friday is our Friday routine of writing whatever you want in your Reader Writer Notebook. Your writings go in the Writing Section.

You can write stories, poetry, or journal entries. You can write a letter to your teacher and ask her questions!

Free Write Friday is about celebrating writing without the pressures of school assignments. This also means it will not be graded for grammar, spelling, or punctuation. This allows you to express your thoughts freely and openly without judgment.

Sometimes, you may not know what to write about. That is okay, too. Every Friday, I try to give you a few ideas that are optional. They are never required, but they help when your brain is too tired to come up with your own ideas. Please know, I love reading your writing. I always write back to you and I get to know you through your work.

As a multi-language learner, your brain is AMAZING! It is difficult to try and write in a new language, but I encourage you to do just that: try. You may also pour your thoughts on the page in your native language. Your thoughts are valuable to me and I do not want language to be a barrier to our connection!

References

Alexander, Kwame. *The Write Thing: Kwame Alexander Engages Students in Writing Workshop (And You Can Too!)*. Huntington Beach, CA: Shell Education, 2019.

Collins, Norma Decker. "ERIC/RCS: Freewriting, Personal Writing, and the At-Risk Reader." Journal of Reading 33, no. 8 (1990): 654–55. http://www.jstor.org/stable/40030533.

Fox, Deborah, and Charles Suhor. "ERIC/RCS Report: Limitations of Free Writing." The English Journal 75, no. 8 (1986): 34–36. https://doi.org/10.2307/819077.

Gallagher, Kelly. *Write like this: teaching real-world writing through modeling & mentor texts*. Portland, ME: Stenhouse Publishers, 2011.

Gallagher, Kelly and Penny Kittle. *180 Days: Two teachers and the Quest to Engage and Empower Adolescents*. Portsmouth: Heinemann, 2014.

Stover, Kim. "Riposte: In Defense of Freewriting." The English Journal 77, no. 2 (1988): 61–62. https://doi.org/10.2307/819521.

www.ingramcontent.com/pod-product-compliance
Lightning Source LLC
LaVergne TN
LVHW081539070526
838199LV00056B/3715